Whit Grace

Whit Grace

Poems by Anne Shivas

Word Poetry

Published by Word Poetry
P.O. Box 541106
Cincinnati, OH 45254-1106

ISBN: 9781625492463

Poetry Editor: Kevin Walzer
Business Editor: Lori Jareo

Visit us on the web at www.wordpoetrybooks.com

Acknowledgements

I am grateful to many people for helpful comments on these poems and encouragement over the years. Fellow poets at the Voices Israel, Jerusalem group and Simon Lichmann and Norman Simms; the Arvon foundation at Lumb Bank and Moniack Mhor, especially Miroslav Holub, George Szirtes, Liz Lochhead and Tom Pow; Doric poet George Bruce; Ray K. Elliott; the poets of the Norwich, Vermont, Library group, the Still Puddle poets and Upper Valley poets Pam Harrison and Don Herzberg; fellow students and staff on the Drew MFA in poetry program, in particular Joan Larkin, Aracelis Girmay, Anne-Marie Macari, Judith Vollmer, Jean Valentine, Gerald Stern and Michael Waters; the Tyne and Esk poetry group and Claire Askew. Special thanks to the "Curry Girls": Jane Seitel, Lori Wilson and Adriana Scopino for fun, friendship and poet-wisdom, and to Sheila Paget and Yvonne Dalziel for their Scottish nous. Many thanks to Jill and Mike Rogoff for help with the literal translation from the Hebrew of "Or" and to Jill for very enjoyable music and poetry collaborations with some of these poems over the years. Thank you again to Pam Harrison for her great poetic instinct, insight, friendship and editing skills. Special thanks to my sister Fiona Shivas for her lovely cover artwork. Lastly huge thanks to all my supportive family and friends, especially my husband Sid Klaus for his continuous encouragement.

I am grateful to the editors of the following magazines and publications in which poems appeared, sometimes in previous forms: *Across Borders*: "An ABC of Praise," *Causeway*: "No Marked Path," *From the Lighthouse*: "What the Shore Said," *Determinations 2*: "Demon of the Deep," *Inspired? Get Writing*: "An Old Woman Cooking Eggs," *Lallans* "Eden Totem," *Northwords Now*: "We Afa Cool," *Osher Anthology*: " Meltwater," *Voices Israel*: "Eve's Garden" and "Sea-Urchin on the Porch, Maine." "What Apollo Said in the Pension Odysseus at Delphi" won second prize in the 1994 Reuben Rose poetry competition. "An Old Woman Cooking Eggs" was runner up in the 2006 National Galleries of Scotland competition. "Time Travel" won the 2016 Tyne and Esk Writer of the Year poetry section.

for Isabel and Andrew Shivas
who gave me the love of music and words

Table of Contents

No Marked Path

Runes Written on the Run

Ask Fit Ail's Ye

ନ୍ଧ ନ୍ଧ ନ୍ଧ ନ୍ଧ ନ୍ଧ ନ୍ଧ ନ୍ଧ

"I like the idea particularly (of)… the writer or the poet being *in receipt*… of messages, just like people listening for stars' messages, astronomers listening…. Nothing is not giving messages, I think."

Edwin Morgan

"I have learned and dismantled all the words in order to draw from them a single word: *Home*"

from "I Belong There" by Mahmoud Darwish, translated by Munir Akash and Carolyn Forche.

No Marked Path

What the Shore Said

I screech, am steep cliff, surging water,
strand, dune and marram grass,
shell and bone hollow, rolled to sand,
spume, white horses' manes on surf,
gannet guzzling mackerel; am blood
anemone, buckies, bladderwrack, kelp,
thrum of a guitar. Upturned empty
crab, blue volcanic scooped out rock,
oyster catcher cooried doon on one leg,
I am crow, hopping. Herring gull, I sail
close to the wind, am sea pink, pink weed,
am snow-strewn, ice sheets cracked,
am an eye, wide open, rooted, children's voices,
fire and song, bud, wee shoals o fish
in slips o waves, broad and flat.
I didn't know un-seeable nets
flip-flops, rose hip, wellie boots,
could be woven around me,
flounder and dog, T-shirts, cagoules.
Salt, gusty, calm, raging, I didn't know
the gods would haul me, dolphin,
porpoise, killer whale, krill back,
pull us in by our dreams.

Demon of the Deep
Blue Hole, Dahab

I am so deep
you will never reach
the end of me;
could lose yourself
in my coral walls,
the living hues
of my edges,
in darting, shimmering
fish that live in nooks and caves
around my broad blue belly.
You could be mine
who forget yourself here,
find you have nothing
in the emptiness of my center.
I could embrace your silent
twist of fear, undress
even your mind.

Sea-Urchin on the Porch, Maine

A palm-sized mound
flecked with silver,
each velvet-sheened,
beveled spine shines.

Smashed open,
it lies, a three-petalled
flower of shell or bone.
In the still white centre

spatula-tongues and arches
bloom where seams of fine
old lace stitch bone to bone
on scales of fish or snake.

Sun and wind-dried
spines loosen, leave
a braille of small white breasts.
It has no use for the sea now.

I carry it to that sparkling edge
cast it back anyway.

Sea Change, Boston

Hot as anguish, these
humid days oppress
us like city towers or fear.
Here kin sleep on streets
arid as bone, beached
on hard shores.
We, too, breathe old air,
suffer inertia's weight
until a thick ocean smell
presses its salt heaviness
inland, reminding us
sea is our first, our liquid
state, and the giant turtle
calls time, to go home.

Roots

On the beach, the ancients—
             the basalt clenched hand,
it's columnar fingers.
From the earth a sulfurous staining stream,
stalactites form over dripping bent,
a web of slow-made stone
             fronts a tiny cave—
our volcanic turbulent past
still bleeding through
             this cooled surface.
In the lee of a west-facing cove,
I lie jet-lagged, eyes closed, on spongy grass,
sheltered from the snell east wind,
             hurtled here, I come to bide,
to let my roots reach deep.

By the Turning Tide

Mother I never knew, every time I see the ocean, every-time
Issa

Knee-deep in sea,
two girls stand at strand's
edge, arms raised
as if in a gesture to calm,

request a moment's
silence, or to receive
rhythms of waves,
wait in still communion—

hands open, palms seaward,
half bare in the sun,
quiet, washed and lapped
by the turning tide,

they address the gannets and gulls,
unseen flatfish, mackerel
and crab—little priestesses
in a time of transmission.

Riding the Head Wind

Aerial artists of wind's high wire—
a hundred feet up and stacked
over shore, wings trimmed to face
the north wind—herring gulls hang poised,

then drop like stones
in some invisible chute, ten,
twenty feet to catch, hold, resume
their quiet equilibrium

until in play with wind and gravity
by a wing's slight turn,
they arc back, wheel
and in air trace a half-moon.

Feather Isle

On Fidra, *Feather Isle*, in Old Norse,
amid the squawking cacophony,

gulls flocking in aerial fields, a young
herring gull hangs dead, head

trapped in the curved loop of a clothes line
left on the long-gone lighthouse keeper's green,

and a downy fledgling has fallen forty feet
from cliff nest to rock, landed among shags

who peck and pull, drive the small gull
to rock's edge: she who has no way to safety,

cannot yet swim or fly, hangs her head—
in her own moment, dies.

Ardi

Happier in the lime trees Ardi
knew her route up with eyes closed—
each foot placement, every hand hold,
where and how to push. Happy to hook knees
over a branch and hang, grass and hedge
upside down, sky the base of her vision.
How she loved the South tree best of all—
every knot and angle, limbs she knew
well as her own small bones. Atop its central
post where two branches grew each
side of a spur she sat secure, arms
round those pillars in a world
of blackbird, thrush and robin. Hours
spent from spring to autumn; first
buds through to winter's bare
frame when ice sprang from pipes
and excursions were short. She lived her love
for this tree, its whorls, wrinkles,
its creases and easy bearing of her.

Advice

a vise will hold wood tight as you saw—
nail a straight cut down—
seal each package well—
save string and tape, paper for tomorrow—

see 360 degrees, not just from a mountain top,
where shale slides under your feet
and learn to surf the hill—

even the keel on a calm run
sails goose-winged, *Mara*'s veil lifted—
did you ever find how many beans make five,

deal with the inner assassin
or bless the times you tried to keep the peace?

Coins Flowed like Water

After the summer
my grandfather died
I became afraid
of the cold certain God
who took him away,
hid deep in sweet
purple lilac or beneath
a yew tree, until tired,
I crept back to the house.
I knew little of death—
but that holiday my father
and brother left Gamrie,
I walked in a vacuum
of sucked-out air.

Our Sooty Grandpa, magician
in whose hands coins flowed
like water between
each knuckle and sponge balls
doubled and disappeared—
the quiet man whose favorite
book was *Huck Finn*,

learned magic in
St. Louis in the twenties,
came back to Aberdeen
with a shiny top hat,
black and white wand—
toured the small towns,
and conjured a rabbit
for a future Queen.

I remember his maroon
armchair by a coal fire,
the children who sat
cross-legged, spellbound,
hushed for shows—
A. Hay Prestowe,
who lit that world,
himself disappeared.

Lines

The Seagull engine unwound
and sputtered under my father's
strong arm, *phut-phut, phut-phut,*
then cast off, *Sea Bear* motored out
between harbor walls to eagle-headed rocks,
Craig and Dargety, gulls squawking
in evenings long as the sky
from horizon to Troupe Head.

My mother hauled creels near rocks—
colored-cork buoys on ropes marked
our own—tossed back small crabs,
hermit crabs, starfish, kept mature
lobster who waved blue-black claws
in fish boxes, curled up their tails.

Later we followed gulls in Gamrie Bay,
put down lines; lead-sinker laden
orange twine, six-hooked, and feathered,
over the gunwales—brought up flashing
sleek silver-blue fluttering mackerel.

Whacked against a bench the fish fell still.
Silver and blood bled into bilges.
White nights stilled.

To the girls, wee Buddhists in the bow,
the boat grew long, sunset
set in stone, red across sky.

Millpond Seas

for Andrew

Like the old ones
who set up muckle stones
we will make
a boat—your body
to ferry, beyond
spirit's gales,
with fine, strong sails,
filled to the gunwales
with hand drums,
mackerel lines,
creels and guns,
big yellow daffodils,
windy day walks on hills,
high blue skies,
millpond seas,
blue, blue cheese,
caviar, crab and *Kummel*,
aniseed balls,
percussive bells and rattles,
picnics on beaches,
black and white films
of old battles,
purring cats,
tail-wagging dogs,
late-night whiskies
with friends,
slow burning logs.
Like your *Maranda* she'll
fare well through
North Sea haar and fogs.

No Marked Path

My true self, my aimless wanderer
Norman MacCaig

I take my mother's strong hand
on the stony beach between
Crovie and Gamrie, and lead her
between rocks and wobbly

stones, a way least hazardous,
where she can follow my foot-
steps as I once followed hers,
where, hand in hand, we collected

wee cowrie shells she kept
in matchboxes and I found
pretty red-white spotted
top shells I loved to death.

Here, where I first became
sure-footed—running leaping
laughing over rocks, a girl-
goat—now I scan the mix

of stone, rock and broken shell
for pottery shards, edges
softened from years of tidal
tumbling, not searching

for anything particular,
not on any marked path,
but knowing the shards
that are mine to pocket,

minding in hand and foot
and eye and heart
the trust in my true self—
my mother's gift.

Shore

This is where I've come to—
where white mist opens on clearings
of rock, wet and sleek as seals
and the heart opens round and soft
as a sea anemone: where whooper swans
fly low, their wings beating
the pulse back to life, and the heron,
once chased at dawn by gulls,
now fishes undisturbed at dusk.

Runes Written on the Run

Eve's Garden, Jerusalem

You would think
this must be
Eve's garden—

so full of fat green figs,
silvery olives, almonds,
whose blossoms like snow signal
small spring, plumping cactus
and sunbirds—flashes of blue
on aloe's fiery flowers.

Summer is ripening peaches, yellow
drops of lemons, walnuts, cherries, round red
pomegranates and plums—each vast night's air
dense with scent of jasmine, rose.

But under summer's fig-
darkened awning steps wind
from *wadi* to the village square,
where children play
games of chance and dare
passing cars,

or indulge
the local passion—
throwing stones.

Delilah

My name is second-hand for *bad*,
but I danced barefoot, ululated
at my wedding—my hips circled
like no other woman's in the room.

Samson kissed these arms three
hundred times from wrist to elbow,
but later how he lied, as our children
were slain by the slings of my tribe.

Sunbird skies turned grey,
Jerusalem stone lost its glow,
hoopoes became afraid,
bulbuls ended their morning song,

grass flamed to ash,
olive, carob trees stood bare,
asphodel bore no blooms,
the Sorek River dried.

At dusk the sky bled onto hills.
This tongue turned to stone in my mouth.
I wish you could see the red I saw.

Elegy for a Small Black Dog
for Hector

Morning, briskly chill,
dogs tussle on Beit Zeit's
mist shore—the loser
rolled in mud or running decked

in drops of light glinting in grass.
Flower children in meadows
return pollen-dusted, yellow petal
strewn, they fall, quick-breathing

in olive's shade. Arriving is good
in the jewel time—sapphire skies,
paths of return—tails raised like flags
signaling good intent. Coy faces greet,

flapping fish tails beat the floor.

§

Now, not wanting to give you to the big man
with slab hands where sheepskins lay, a mass
of meat and sprawling limbs, I cradle your head
in the green shroud, help lower you into the wheelbarrow.

The Masks
Jerusalem, 1991

In taut days before war,
all tourists gone,
Dead Sea road deserted
bar armored cars,
we make a sealed room.
Tape plastic bags over windows.
Inside we ready towels, water
to create a gas excluder
for the door gap,
to keep out poison gas,
mustard gas. We add snacks,
stacked tins of fruit,
beans, Israeli champagne.
Downtown we fill forms,
paperwork for foreigners
to pick up masks in a muckle
warehouse—a gey lang wait
for plain brown boxes
and a mask near identical
to the black rubber
horse-head long-kept
by my grandmother
in a wooden chest.
We take the masks
when we go out.

Jerusalem Threads

Driving east and down to the Dead Sea,
webs of trails, fine threads
of brown dust like cat's cradles
lie over hills—a riddle solved
by loose groups of goats grazing
round boys in bright shirts—
Bedouin on sandstone rocks with sticks.
I find the same pattern from sheep's feet
on Canna's banks in Scotland's thick
resilient green—*coming back*—I see—
so many pathways through the spring grass.

Christ in the House of Mary and Martha

after the painting by Johannes Vermeer

Arriving, Jesus was tired. In brutal heat
and dust, children on the road,
running beside him, shiny-eyed,
offered fennel seeds to chew,

but now he was weary of crowds.
We washed his feet, prepared a basin
of cool water, fresh herbs, a soft
cloth, and Martha wiped away dirt

from between his toes and the sole's skin
softened despite dry, baking days
of walking. Knowing there was no need
for words among friends, he slept

as we prepared food. Martha boiled
and ground chick-peas for hummus,
rolled falafel, while I cooked
fresh flat bread over a fire. We ate olives,

soft sheep's cheese, figs and drank mint tea.
Day cooled into evening,
the house stones still warm,
we talked, and I sat at Jesus' feet

when Martha brought special leavened
bread in a basket, to celebrate his being
here—women like you know—he said
love changes us; kindness, a blanket given,

a glass of water, a meal, makes
miracles, makes us hearty and hale.

What Apollo Said in the Pension Odysseus at Delphi

Stay and rest—
let the new moon wax
to full, and sing
overtones
round this valley.

Leave behind
heaving, crashing waves,
mad running, sailing,
wind in your hair.

Play your harp,
oil your feet,
brush your hair.
Let the sea-born moon
rise above
the barefoot sun.

East, the snaking flute
winds in rocky valleys,
between islands, across

the sea. West is more
somber tuned, a straight
widening sound.

Stay and rest.
Feel my breath.
Hear my speech.

An Old Woman Cooking Eggs

after the painting by Diego Velazquez

That's me in the painting.
My face smooth and brow clear,
for I do not worry over
what I cannot see. My
hands rough with
washing, scrubbing,
rubbing, my arms strong
from carrying children,
water, melons.

Do you see how I fry eggs?
I gently nudge and push that
soft translucent smear
to move the whitening mass,
feel how they are done.
On the table beside garlic sit
stinging peppers that burn my eyes,
milk in jugs worn soft by hands.

That's my grandson.
They say he has a shadow
across his brow, looks always to the side
as if, if he could turn his head
a little bit further, he might see
what troubles him.

I know the steadiness of his arm,
the even sound of his step.
My hands know his smooth moon face.

Rock by Rock

after paintings by Australian Aboriginal women
in *Dreaming Their Way*, 2007

From far away
across the earth,
sisters of animals
and stars,

bring an ancient order—
grasses, waterholes,
summer swathes of flowers,
know each tree, each rock.

From a life without walls,
you map stories
to navigate the world,
draw important knowledge

of food and spirit—
where they are found,
how they came to be.
You show wind

moving through,
bending, spiniflex grass,
chart the course
of a dry river bed.

You place stars
in a night sky,
envision a single hair—
drop by drop,

you set down rain,
rock by rock,
bush by bush,
paint the earth.

You daub points of joy—
beads that link back
to dreamtime,
to your own kin.

In Vermont

I meet the rhythms of my ancestors
   in a low-roofed cape, hear honey-splash
   of polished harps, weaving of flute
and lute over chairs, oriental rugs.
   Beside the loom, a map, and summer's
   destination written on yellow tabs—
Mallaig, Badachro, Inverewe. The hum
   of voices, percussion of forks on plates
   drifts away: *Pennan, Gamrie, Macduff.*

Labor Day, Maine

Wheeze of saws, sander's reel,
places with my people's names:
Latham, Nisbet, McDonald, Lowe.
Summer work, painting sides,
sills, as Fall's first leaves lie
red on new-paved roads. In cars
with plates from other states
visitors go—leave the silver-
hammered sea. We arrive late
to catch September's diamond days,
pink corn moon, eat last punnets
of blueberries, brambles,
savor the Pemaquid River,
empty, save blue herons,
painted turtles warming backs
on rocks, broken branches.
I read on the porch, watch
monarch butterflies mass
on bushes by St John's Bay,
move south on windless air.
How fast barn's shingles grey
weather-side! A balsam fir
planted under telephone wires
has made a complex dance
of undulation—to grow tall,
a bit to the side—made a slow
body-swerve, shift, as we sometimes must, just off-centre.

Fall River Life, Maine

As we paddle
kayaks on the Pemaquid
river   mirror
to cerulean sky,
cumulus drift below
red hulls,
are split
by the upturned V of our glide.

Painted turtles
warm backs
and heads   black necks
stretched to sun,
they perch
on dark stubs
of wood—
take no notice of our quiet slide.

Single pond skaters
leave clear
zig-zag   trails
while wild groups
carve circles,
curve
at a crazy pace.

On wings
that have no need
to beat   sails
an osprey—
over straight,
traces
a surveyor's sight-line.

Herons
have mostly flown
though one   young
or frail,
forms an upturned L
of neck, head, beak
that peeks
between grass spiders' filament streams.

Before we take
our crab-like exits
a blue heron   cruises by—
great gun-metal grey
grave display of flight,
huge wings
barely beat
as she slices through the silence at our side.

November Arrhythmia

On a screen of clouds a rising
sun spreads white gold

and orange, the river below,
motionless, dark.

Students, all legs beneath a rowing-shell,
no heads, scuttle; a human

centipede. *Strange Spring* has come
in new primrose, dandelion,

—a week ago under snow.
Warm now we sit out

at a cafe in town—
winter has missed   a beat.

Broth

On a dreich day
I cook soup,
seek sustenance
in golden orange
of butternut squash,
cut cubes to trim
thick skin, drop
in a blue pot with peach
yam, purple onion,
a still crisp apple, dust
in green rosemary,
marbled nutmeg.
Bright lumps birsle
in oil as edges soften,
release nostril-
opening scent
of sweet hillside
summer. Hotter
in green stock
then birl to a silk-sheen
of amber brose—
drink deep,
color bleak
November bones.

Winter Song

Leaves of ice

A sure sign of coming winter—
earth opens dark cones,
sprouts spears of ice, curling
over, twisting, grown
in the first hard frost.

First Snow

Fine first snow dusts
leaves on the forest floor:
each shape, maple or oak,
frosted stiff, iced, crisp,
the ground a layered tray
of browned leaf biscuits.

Stems of ice

Squat stems of ice like rows of dwarfs
with pointed hats and lace trimmed skirts,
or tapered hand-dipped candles, pendants
of etched glass, hang on ice-sleeved branches—
a corrieneuchin burn with crystal elephant feet.

Late Snow

Snow on trees
forms ribbons, loops,
and drapes over branches—
like long white adders,
their bodies falling
in garlands.

Crinkled, snow swatches
are rouched and drawn
in waves—
a concertina
of peaks and troughs—
in winter we coorie in,
gang up an doon.

Wind Slams a Lion's Paw

Early morning,
        trees sheathed and sleeved
                in silver ice, milky hush,
earth's breath close,
        on the windshield,
                wind slams a lion's white paw.

On the frozen river,
        storm-dusted,
                mackerel-backed,
Djinns twist high
        white funnels,
                and criss-cross

turkey V's
        of back-country skis
                mark the hill.
Against fences' staves
        dried notes rise,
                ghost flowers of fall—

the field a slate of runes
        written on the run—
                deer, snowshoe rabbit
coyote, fox,
        parallel tracks—
                hieroglyphs
of faa and faar we are.

Meltwater

Like deep tides drawing away,
snow recedes, reveals
rocks, stones, a sandy strand

of winter brown, grass long
hidden under the flood.
Crazy paving pieces of ice

float white down the dark
Connecticut river affirming
winter's sure break-up

here and in the North. On old
maples sap buckets appear,
our walks on warming days

punctuated *tap tap tap*
by running sap. Only we
who live in cold latitudes

really know this blessing—
feeling a year's first mildness
after brutal cold, the change

from our northern dragon's
burning breath, like entering
a sanctuary, finding rest.

From pond's lip, meltwater
spills; its cries heard
by the blood, its gush and heart.

Spring Song

In March we count
                    flowers,
On the ides   two crocus prayers
                            three snowdrops,

on the seventeenth,
St Patrick's day,   bees between,
                    they open bell-stars to the sun,
                            and nothing has eaten them.

Make no major decisions in March or April, Sarah,
            the horse-woman warned,
                    when we first came north—

            weakened by lack of sun and heat
                        we do not think straight,
we are   pale yellow things, daffodil shoots
                        grown flat   askew
below stones   piles of dead leaves.

 I see the Goddess in each tree   sinuous dancer
                                    many-armed
though February's storm
        splintered, cracked, wrenched
                    she opens her green hands—
            like Kali, crushes   the demon
                            beneath her feet.

Beware of love
it holds a danger   of losing yourself—
                            you do not know if
you   will return.

March Day

Ice floes glide down the brown Ottaquechee.
Ompompanoosuc gushes, spurts in spate,
frost heaves like standing waves toss cars.

In fields dappled as a ptarmigan in winter molt
a snowshoe hare is half-way to summer coat.
No need for lights beneath an Equinox

full moon, or hats, jackets, gloves
in Spring's warm flush as roof ice releases,
crashes and wild-eyed horses bolt.

A Hebridean Day on the Hill, Vermont

Rain falls in rows, rank on rank.

Fence, bare bone branches,
swollen buds all strung
with liquid Perspex drops.

Far views are lost in drifts-of-mist.
I hear water's percussion—
retort of rain on a metal roof,
swish and rush of streams, the *tick*,

tick, beat on my Goretex jacket hood.

Mottled Month

The North's own season of mottled mud
and melt, sugar snow, ruts on washboard roads;
first southern returnees, red-wing blackbirds
perch in apple trees, pronounce tri-syllabic whirrs

as ground gives under boots and green shows up
from winter dun in dusty light—it comes
our way on March long days, a mess of dirt
we trail into houses, towel off dogs.

We've made it through! Faces stretch to smiles.
But winter's a tease, plays us like a yo-yo,
hangs on too long; stains magnolia cups
brown, blows cold and hot, like a chancy

friend, until we don't know where we are,
wonder if it will ever end—get used to it.

Mass

Frogs croak their presence in April sun seeking
mates, their green eyes beading the vernal
pool. Clasped they lie like charms on rims
of Burmese drums and leave tight black bundles
of spawn, loosening in time to sprawled sponge
sacks—the pond now a nursery
for dark flecks feeding, wriggling their tails.
But May rains do not come this year and soon
the pool shrinks, grows crowded, tadpoles roll,
turn pale bellies up, push heads out
as if for air in a bare puddle,
layer of tadpole on tadpole. Still no rain
and all dries, flies buzz round the limp mass
of grey bodies, smell of death fills the air.
I take my spade, step in the mud, cover them.

Sustenance

Jet trails linger in high skies
as I lie on the dock of a pond

listening for plop of fish
or purr of dragonfly

close to my cheek or bleat
of a sheep from its field.

Maples and oaks round this lip
of pond are tinted ripe as peaches,

raspberries. Birches pulse like lemons,
little burn babbles its constant

murmur and gurgle. Shoes and socks
off I dip feet and legs in cool dark

turn onto my stomach, stir and sieve
water with fingers and hands.

I bathe eyes, lids closed, in Fall's
blaze and incandescent glow.

Ask Fit Ail's Ye

An Wi Whit Grace

Fish-hook sharp,
lochan deep,
she holds her peaty vision
dark in the pupil
of her eye,
no reflected sky.

Jet and far as space,
as full of light,
the gleg n spark,
Scottish child
div ye ken yer place
in the universe?
Faar's hame?

Ye hiv tae keep sayin
it's aricht
it's nae sae bad
whit wis hale
wisnae ever broken.

Here you know
the lie of the land.

Faan she wis a fish
a flick o her tail
freed her.

The warld unfurls
itsel
like a bolt
o fabric
in Remnant Kings
or a wind-whipped Saltire.

She's looking back
tae afore 1707
mebbe een tae
a Pictish time
twa thoosan years ago.

Doon deep
in the Caledonian wood
whit a bonny
diversity—
the adder coiled
asleep on sun-lit
path, nae feart,
though watchfu,
through its peaty eye.

An wi whit grace does it uncoil itsel,
lead head first in lang successive loops
intae the thick grass an tangle o hawthorn
aneath the muckle an zagging oaks.

Scottish child,
ye hiv tae pay attention,
tak care an mind how ye go,
ask fit ails ye.

§

On a high road above the Strathmore Vale
she traces the snake with her finger, its meander
incised along the top of an Aberlemno stone.
It's Pictish kin the golden sea-god unfurls,
part snake or fish and dragon, flies from towers
and church spires in Brechin and Kirriemuir.

§

Wis it a totem, the python bag, her mither carried?
Soft, smooth the scales stroked one way, catchy
the ither, *sae lik oursels*. The girl would steal
in sometimes to her mother's room, just to sit
with this snake, touch its skin, her eye held
by black on grey shapes, the bag snapped shut.
She wis aye careful not tae malagruize.
Tho we were nivver meant tae be tae guid,
dark and stiff as an Auld Kirk Elder,
nivver meant tae deny oursels owre much.

It wisnae the weemun an snakes
faa cleared us oot o Eden
it wis the mannies wi their chain-
saws an trucks faa cut it aa doon.

The Light Room

I found the hidden source of light
after some looking. My interest sown
in Lucy's home and a room
so bright it made me strangely calm.

I thought my house must have one too.

High above the entrance
sweep of stair, a paneled
glass ceiling ended my gaze,
draped walls in long rhomboids of light.

I found a door on the third floor,
three feet high, behind a broad chest
of drawers. Alone, I edged the chest aside
then needing no key, opened the door

where glass ceiling became floor—
a white-walled room, soaring
cupola above. I sat in silent awe
tucked in the doorway, steeped in light.

Enchantress

As a girl, I thought
my mother had magical powers—

an inborn, untaught
way to talk to flowers

so each in turn
would tell its name—

primrose, celandine,
hare bell, wild thyme.

School

was long days,
a well of echoing stairways

and uniform

until free at three
like sycamore seeds

I took mind's wing, and flew.

birds?

emulate

to

wish

the   sky   for   light

like   trees   reach   for

lifting   do   its   words

its   poems   like   spires
script   that   builds
Is   there   a
into   some   well?
a   precipice
an   edge
falling over
climbing not
than descent
a prayer—
aspiration
more ascent
buildings
more as
were made
if poems

How Would It Be

Kith and Kin

She's a kindred spirit,
Janet, soul sister
in New England—
shares kennels, farmer's market,
the free school, Inter-
faith Thanksgiving,
where a snowy night she says
her grandmother
sailed from Scotland,
settled in Nova Scotia,
was called *McLaren*—
my own family name.
We *are* kin—heirs
of fine skin, thin hair,
a deep air; we hail
from the earth
of Perth and Angus

In a Name

I	am		
Anne,			
Anne	I		am,
that is	Anne,		
like	ran	not	van
can		not	fan
no	man	but	*femme*,
not	tan	or	ban
more	Pan	than	Nan
not	nae	or	nane
but	aye	my	ane.

Words

My father spoke two languages—
one for family, fellow doctors,
surgeons of the Royal College,
Edinburgh neighbors—anither

fir spikkin tae auld friends
fae Aiberdeen, The Broch,
Pe'erheid, Gamrie or Crovie.
He slid between two tongues

in the Nor'east, or at hame
haivan a guid blether on the wall phone
ootside the bathroom wi Charley, Birnie
or Johnson, Beatrice or Leila.

'Oh its yersel' 'Fit like', 'Aye nae bad'
'Aye the bairns are all doin fine at school'
where there were words we dared not use—
words sic as *scunner, semmit, fiel* or *fou.*

Thochts

I didn't know the dangers
of the *shan gadgie*
whose words I'd fain have kennt
I couldnae trust,
but, och, I'd been taught tae think
his thochts meant mair than mine.

Fit Dis Wur Semmit

Scared to say—
Fit dis wur semmit
haf tae dae wi the Jews
an the war? I chose
silence over a red face—

learned in one eight-week block
the Scots lost at Culloden,
though it was a mystery
whit for we were fighting.

I went south,
after college—
jobs, more degrees,
though I *wunnered*
sometimes *faa* the English
were *spikkin tae*—
looked *ower* my shoulder,

found my Scottish banknotes
turned down by a man
in an ice-cream van—
nae wunner in summer
I cheered as I crossed
the border, *came hame*.

We Afa Cool

After *We Real Cool* by Gwendolyn Brooks

We afa cool. We
skive school. We

lirk late. We
nip neat. We

lo'e lust. We
bet bust. We

jag June. We
deid soon.

Mayor

After *Mayor* by Yehuda Amichai

Fit sair
tae be Mayor o Jerusalem.
Fit a sair trachle.
Foo can ony man be mayor o sic a city?

Fit can he dae wi it?
He maun big, an big, an big.

An ae nicht
the stanes o the hills roon aboot
maun raik doon
till the stane hooses
lik wolves comin
tae yowl at the dugs
faa hiv become thirled tae men.

Or

After *Before* by Yehuda Amichai

Or the gate is shut
or aa the questions hae bin askit
or I am changit.
Or the bluid o a wise man clots
or aathing's pit awa i the press
or the mortar hairdens.
Or aa the chanter-holes are blockit
or we unnerstaun aa the rules
or we braak aa the tools.
Or the law is enakit
or God shuts his haun
or we gang awa frae here.

Strivin tae Be above Masel

After *Ambition* by Robert Creeley

Couldnae jaloose it
couldnae thole it—

wisnae ever
thar then. Winnae

cam back, dinnae
need it.

Sonnet

After *Sonnet* by Terence Hayes

We blew our own bagpipes into balloons
We blew our own bagpipes into balloons
We blew our own bagpipes into balloons
We blew our own bagpipes into balloons
We blew our own bagpipes into balloons
We blew our own bagpipes into balloons
We blew our own bagpipes into balloons
We blew our own bagpipes into balloons
We blew our own bagpipes into balloons
We blew our own bagpipes into balloons
We blew our own bagpipes into balloons
We blew our own bagpipes into balloons
We blew our own bagpipes into balloons
We blew our own bagpipes into balloons

Eight Questions for My Nose

When you bled dark,
thick in my seventh
year, was the blood
my mother's? Nasal
bones removed
to clear her sinus
she misses the nose,
I now wear.
Could I lend you back
for a few days,
a month in lilac time?
Are you a Highland nose,
my *Schiehallion*—a *sron*,
leading best by loch-
side, thistle-lined tracks
where larks rise?
Is the middle of a face
a good home, infection's
danger zone? As trouble
walked toward my door,
did you smell it?
Where is my nous, nose?
What turns you up
or down, makes
your nostrils flare?
What gives you
the heart to dare?

Ode to a Food Processor

Kitchen's whiz
s-blade curls
to whirl and birl
soup to smooth
puree, to crunch
nuts, commit
bread to crumb,
alchemize flour
and butter
to powder
for pastry.
You turn
banana liquid
smash, crash
icy blueberries
on crucible
sides, smooth
yogurt drinks
in silence.
Whirr of carrot
grated, parsley
pulsed,
thrum, thrum
of flour gathered
in a rolling ball,
you keep *mum*
in the corner,
are shifty—
is it a *sair affront*—
the outbursts,
raucous noise?

The Gift

Set in a chiffonier,
the porcelain *bierstein*
celebrated Greta's
German grandfather's
return from war—
a child, her fingers
traced bas-relief
beer garden scenes.
My Bombardier,
Royal Field Artillery,
grandfather was gassed,
his lungs nivver the same.
Did these men
line up against
the other
over dreich fields—
baith lads then
ordered tae kill?
Mine now, I make
a small memorial,
charge the *bierstein*
with water,
float a candle.

Guy Fawkes Night

Under a mussel sky, low cloud
membranes diffuse moon light—

forgotten shadow puppets
staid in a pageant of fire

we draw night's silence into us.

Listen, Now
for Bani Shorter

In the crematorium the Ajahn
splashes water over us, burns dried sage
in a gaping bowl. You are with us, but gone.
Bright star, whom the Ajahn calls *Great
Spirit*, you became so light, bold wind
near blew you whose gift was *listen, now.*
We speak of your attentiveness as we touch
the white coffin, then *allowing*, your form slides on.
Woman whose wisdom is balm to prisoners,
murderers and the good, released to clear skies—
we are gathered here by train and plane,
this once together, do you hear us?

Soifitis

The first symptom
appeared
on her computer screen
in words runtogether,
nospacesbetweenlongstrings
like 'gottosee' or 'wewillcall.'
Next she noticed
somethingsimilar
withherbreath,
nobreathingspace
leftbetweenactivities,
longphraseswithnopauses,
and then
a gulp
of air
asifbeforegoingdown
somewhere deep.
Then she got really sick
as if her body simply needed
to correct the growing compression,
the runningtogether and
strangeconjoining—
to give things back their
proper pace, value and measure.
No music without the spaces,
the jazz players say,
no breathing in
if not
breathing out—
itdoesn'thavetobejustgotthrough,
ye dinna hae tae thole it lass.

Shine the Kettle Drums

Shine the kettle drums with Brasso for half
an hour until light blooms on their dun sides.
No sin not to finish—they'll be that way for years.
Save your days for *Kick the Can*.
                              Music of the fish
van draws your mother out to the street, spares
her a hise to the fishmonger.
                              Eating honey fresh
from the hive, comb's yellow cells on toast,
boiled blue eggs from hens the sax-player rears,
you hear Monday night's jazz playing them sane.

Time Travel

I have come back:
squeak of cast iron gate,
pass post box beneath
a lime tree arch
where my eyes lift,
follow the bike ramp
to the side of steps—
my shoulders, hands know
the push and grip of steep ascent.
A sweep of stone wings,
an open river of domestic rock,
leads to yellow door, mosaic floor;
a flood of blackbird song
in summer's late light.
A girl in tennis white
I enter what was once home
to pick up glasses
I'll not need until
years from now,
and take a thick book—
Mandela's song,
years before he writes
or I discover
the rough blue walls,
of my Calvinist prison,
or find the need
to sing freedom's song,
kin-song; find
the right tone
to break walls.

Brummle Eatin

After *Blackberry Eating* by Galway Kinnell

I lu'e tae gae oot at summer's end
atween the sonsie, cauld black brummles
tae eat brummles first thing i the morn
the stems gey jagged, a pey
they gat fu kennin yon black airt
o brummle makkin; an as I staun atween them
pu'ing the stems tae ma mou, the saftest anes
fa near as magic tae ma lip
jist as words afttimes dae, antrin words
lik *sowans, squische* and *squeenge*
mony-lettered, ane syllable junts
that I squishe, pleiter an squatter
in yon still, feart, cranreuch cauld tongue
o brummle eatin at summer's end.

An ABC of Praise

Praise Alba, acorns, aleph, ancestors, apes and Ardi

Praise bells, bugles, bangles, books, Ben Lawers and brambles

Praise Crovie, children, chocolate, candles, crepes and camels

Praise daisies, delphinium and dogs, desert, dreams, dancing

Praise elbow, espaliers, Eigg, elephant and eyes, echo

Praise forests, friends, fire, feet, flute, fall and feather

Praise grapes, gloves, grace, giggles, girls and granite

Praise hand, hearth, hips, humor, Holly and hope

Praise islands, Iona, inwardness, instinct, intuition and ink

Praise jam, juniper, jellyfish and June, Jerusalem, jasmine

Praise kites, kulfi, kisses, kayaks, keels and kilts

Praise ladybirds, lilies and lochs, lapdogs, loons, lyric, *laldie*

Praise Maine, Merlin, mothers, minaret, milkweed and
                                                    metronome

Praise names, nous, nose, notes, and northern lights, nooks

Praise oatcakes, oars, osprey and olives, outrigger, owl

Praise paint, pencils, poems, paper, ptarmigan, puffin and
                                                    platypus

Praise quail, quilts, quince, quartz, *queans* and Qumran

Praise rakes, rays, reeds, reels, rings and ripples

Praise skis, squash, snow and silliness, shells, Socrates, sun

Praise turtles, tennis, tents, teeth, triskelia and thistle

Praise umbelates, ululation, sea-urchin and up-beat, up-take,
                                                        unison

Praise Vermont, volcanoes, valentines, vanilla, vertebrae and
                                                        vegetarians

Praise words, woods, waves, water, whales and *whin*

Praise xylophones, x-rays, Xerox, xylographs and xanthous

Praise yams, yachts and Yosemite, yew, yurts, Ygdrasil

Praise zebra, zabaglione, the zodiac, zithers, zips, Zen and
                                                        Zebedee

Little Neighbors

Little neighbors I said to them, where is my tomb?
Garcia Lorca

Small snouting
craiturs, sisters
of moles
and worms,
gatekeepers
of the unseen,
will you whisper
to me when it is time,
catch at my ear, stall
my moving with a cold finger
pressed to its tip,
deliver your secret
news from cool lips,
passing ear's pinna
as warm mist rises
from earth's vents
on chilly days?
Will you touch
my wing-
blades,
herd me
to earth?

Notes on the Poems

Ardi — The title of this poem comes from an early pre-human ancestor whose skeleton was found in Ethiopia, and was named Ardipithecus ramidus, Ardi for short.

Millpond Seas — *Kummel* is an aniseed flavored German liqueur.

Shore — This poem was inspired by the poem "Sea" by Finnish poet Bo Carpelan from *Rooms Without Walls*, translated by Ann Born. The first line of that poem begins "Here's where I've come to…"

Eve's Garden, Jerusalem — *wadi* is the Arabic term for a valley.

Jerusalem Threads — The italicized lines at the end of the poem are from a Haiku by Buson, translated by Yuki Sawa and Edith M. Shiffert.

An Wi Whit Grace? — In the Scots of Aberdeenshire an "F" often replaces the "Wh" sound of a question. *Faar* is where, *Fan* is when, *Fit* is what, *Div* is do.

Mayor — Translated from the Hebrew by Assia Guttman and Ted Hughes

Or — Mike and Jill Rogoff helped me greatly with the finer points of the literal translation from the Hebrew.

Glossary of Scots Words

Aye, ae	always, every
ane	a certain person, someone
antrin	odd, peculiar, strange
bairn	child
baith	both
bent	coarse grass
big	build
birsle	scorch, warm thoroughly
birl	revolve rapidly, whirl round, dance
blether	chat
brose	traditional Scottish dish of oat or pease meal, golden in color
brummle	blackberry
buckie	edible whelk
burn	stream
cagoule	lightweight waterproof jacket
coorie doon	bend, lower, snuggle or fold in
corrieneuchin	conversing intimately
craitur	creature, critter
cranreuch	hoar-frost
div	do
dreich	of weather; dreary, bleak, hard to bear
faa	who
faan	when
faar	where
fiel	a fool, foolish
fit	what
fou	drunk
gey	very
gleg	quick, keen in perception
haar	sea mist or fog
jaloose	wish for, be jealous

junts	large piece of something, especially meat or bread
laldie	do something exuberantly, vigorously
malagruize	dishevel, disarrange, spoil
maun	must
muckle	large in size, big, great
or	ere, before
ower	over
pey	punishment, chastisement
pleiter	idly or aimlessly make a mess with, dabble
queans	girls
raik	straggle, wander through
Saltire	Scottish flag
Schiehallion	prominent centre point and Scottish mountain in Perthshire: Gaelic name translates as Fairy Hill of the Caledonians
scunner	aversion, disgust, loathing
semmit	undershirt or vest, usually of wool or flannel
shan gadgie	untrustworthy, unknown person
snell	of weather; biting, bitter, severe
sonsie	plentiful, hearty, plump
sowans	dish from oat husks and fine meal used in fermentation process
squatter	squander, scatter about
squeenge	prowl or slink about
squische	crush, squash
sron	Scottish Gaelic: nose, name of some hills in the highlands
stane	stone
thirl	indentured servant
thole	bear, endure, suffer
till	to
trachle	exhaust with overwork, overburden, struggle
whit	what
whin	common furze or gorse bush
yowl	cry, roar, shout, howl